Hummingbird Quay

Caroline Arbelay

Presentation by *BookLeaf Publishing*

Web: www.bookleafpub.com

E-mail: info@bookleafpub.com

ISBN: 978-93-95784-11-5

First edition 2022

DEDICATION

Para Mami.

april parts I and II

i slouched through
april pulling on the pound of
worry like a soft down coat.
i want peace
on my door. i want nothing
breathing. nothing
at my walls.
i left
my dreams safe on the ground close
by the willow tree
to weep or pick or pluck
a clean note through
my yellow childhood
and my orange good.
//
don't call her by that name
she doesn't wear it anymore
in pocket universes she is more herself than she
has ever been
nobody mourns that girl you used to know

she holds her soul a little straighter now

gifted
how that word clambered in her ear and made a
home there
but wasn't that the last time she belonged and
doesn't she miss it

and in pocket universes she is more herself than
she has ever been
and fat or skinny envelopes don't hold a flame
about her skin
how many times must she begin to balance
memory and hope and
life as it turned out

don't call her by that name
she doesn't wear it anymore
but

she still wears flannel shirts and words fall down
her sleeves just like before

us

we get used
to our infirmities
and fail to seek out cures
we sit on our comfortable lies
and slide into oblivion

un needed
un-tended
unfed

vary

us your tender words
we've heard them all before
vary our experience
our ways
our days
our wrongs

and please somebody look for
us

it's not been done before

deliver us

merciless sunshine
warm sand on winter shoes
deliver us

hot broken pavement
cracked walls and endlessness
deliver us

history history
elderly footfalls and worry
deliver us

legs in the water
dark salt and native sea
deliver me

into the promise of autumn
where color gets blown apart
body and soul keep together

deliver us
far from my ice-flecked heart

bus

i look out through a spotty window
air-conditioned speeding by
i see my glory and my past
i see my large and clever cast
i see my crumbling grandeur
home and homelessness
miles per hour speeding by
that laughing lagoon and this rocky shore
measure
the span of my heart nothing more
we ride by air-conditioned miles per hour
the taste of my tongue is sour
could-haves dancing on her tip i
slip beneath our crackling sun
down a shot of bus exhaust
ancient cobbles drawing near
wide with worry i
step out into my bright bright lies

untitled

the heat rains down
in white sun glitter
I am washed of my comfort

the trees swoosh and dance in a
toothless breeze

even the birds sound tired in their
song today
waiting on fountains and delight

and degree by degree I am less
myself
chatter chatter clanging in my brain

rushing and all I want
is sleep
until the coolness of spring wakens
me

and I remember crisp white curtains
billowing into the kitchen
and I can smell fresh cut grass

blackout

the whoosh of trees is worrisome
this creaky futon heat won't leave my bones

snap quiet the ceiling fans click off
clack noise the tick of clocks roll by

sloop a hose dribbles outside
the silence is so loud

full of insects thoughts and engines
the torpor gains its mark

tinkle an ice cream cart trundles
coconut drips down my tongue

i wait for the dark
and the promise of coolness which never comes

kites

bright triangles
footfalls on grass
glitter-blue sea

these old walls have watched

squeals of joy
coconut ice cream
dogs on their evening constitutionals

these old walls have watched

worry and delight and
lost souls welcome here
the corners of the night enveloping

these old walls have watched

trudging down the road
shrinking day
stray cats staring out from their plastic houses

these old walls have watched

down down down

music promising to clean the silence from your
ears
stuff your mouth with street food
and hollow out your tears

bright triangles floating out to sea
sometimes they seem to be the only
things these walls have ever seen

gray

grainy gray day
author of my soul
come rest in me

cold rain
cool my skin and the ire within

i am invisible
clean my rage

i am unstoppable
free my gaze from the past and the future
and through wet lashes let me see this moment
as it is

full of books and music
furry blue and white socks and hair thrown up in
a careless bun

waterlogged leaves and heavy branches
grainy gray day
author of my soul come
rest in me

WBY

we are all stories
what have you got against that
is your imagination so limited
that you can't smile at my turn of phrase face

I am a novel
A book of poetry
A West End musical

does that make me any less real than you think
you are
all hard syllables and judgement

My heart has been formed by
William Butler Yeats

who wrote you?

Reverence

shimmer sky
swishing trees that sound like ladies' dresses at a
ball
dancing shadows on tree trunks
dancers' limbs
i point my toes to join in nature's revelry
sunlight on rooftops
glimmering windows
people go about their business like shades within
i do not join them
i am invisible
a breeze caressing faces in a crowd
i am invincible
the life breath and blood in everything around
me
old tree limbs twirl me
i want to be those ladies' dresses
smashing through doorways
crashing through walls
limber arms circle circle
dizzy footfalls fizzy brain
i point my toes
to join in the Reverence
bow to the dance
with reverence and mirth

humdrum daze

I am not that humdrum creature
marching through the day
stacking minutes stacking hours
as if they were real

I am wild abandon
I am burnished steel

I am not that humdrum creature
slouching through the day
counting minutes counting hours
inching out of ease

I am a cloudless blue sky
I am the shifting autumn breeze

I am not that humdrum creature
crouching come what may
willing minutes willing hours
to pass along out of my way

I am an estuary sweet
and salty air
I am the month of January
all my limbs laid bare

unsewn

i blur the edges
to my barbed wire soul
and pretend these wasted years
haven't made me old

i pick at the seams
of my weary heart
and call it art

rage dances on my tongue
she dances till i'm drunk
on all the bitterness
i earned when i was young

rage beats against my eyes
as memories rise and fall
i knew that i was right
i thought i knew it all

and am i angry now
and am i angry still

i pick at the seams of my weary heart
and call it art

what's it to you

What makes you think
you can put a smile on my face?
When did I ever give you
permission to try?
Do you think you have
that kind of power?
Well, let me disabuse you
of that notion right now.

I own my mirth
and my ruthlessness.
My eyes and mouth
crinkle at my own thoughts.
I smirk at my leisure.
I am not prey to your manipulation.
I laugh for my pleasure.
I do not need your aid or validation.

I own my mirth
and my ruthlessness,
my rage
and its fruitlessness.
And if I choose
to bare my teeth
or wear a sullen mask,

what's it to you?

the third grade

i was never scared of the wind
when I was little
i was only scared of everything in the third grade
i cried at the big fat substitute and they sent me to the
counselor's office
where i learned that my nature was wrong
no, i was never afraid of the wind
i was only scared of the slide in kindergarten
and i made everyone behind me climb back down the
ladder when
i changed my mind at the top
my friend Elbert remembered and brought it up
senior year
but i was never afraid of the wind
and there were days when it blew the kitchen curtains
in,
spring days
and there were days it clanged the park swings in the
sun
and there are days when it sparks the autumn leaves
to riotous
dance
but now cold summer winds remind me of hurricanes
and cold summer winds remind me of waterless
shores
and cold summer winds remind me of green-ocean
rainwater
up to my knees

the digital times

a string pulls us together
tight around round bellies flat stomachs and
overarching guts
we are gut willed
and dance and rest ourselves in digital arms
our aching souls craving
glistening meals we've hardly ever tasted
love freedom connection

in our private fiefdoms
the food is stale
hardened by our hearts' syncopated beats
our lack of breath and room and daring

so we hang tight to this string
all red fingers and white nails
and dance dance
until we collapse
weary and full and perhaps new
into digital arms

inauthentic b****

inauthentic you call me
how dare you
when my dumb earnestness brought me here

beat down
rigid
wouldn't you be if you held all my fear
carried it down all these years
heavy with my bones

spoiled you call me
what do you know of my spite
to let your half hearted consonants and vowels
define me
your nonsense syllables unwind me

and do you think
your so called fire will refine me

how arrogant

and how dare you
how DARE you
call anyone worthless

impractical things

cool grey breeze
a ceiling fan
wasted yellow longings

chill her ears
she wants

impractical things

she dreamed about ancient things
the night before
such old want

and new attention

and now she wants utterly

impractical things

for m

she said that she wants to belong
i want to tell her that she only needs to belong to
herself

but strangers take money
and strangers pour honey

on wounds that have lasted a lifetime
but then i'm not being honest myself
i want to belong and i've ridden along
on this ride that she started but can't seem to stop

and strangers take money and strangers pour
honey

on scars
that were never their own
so how could they know

that i don't need their salve anymore
and i wish i could tell her that she only needs to
belong to herself
and i wish i believed it myself

little red cart

she pushes along her little red cart
leaning creaking bending seeking solace
for aging

she shuffles along this well worn track
lean creak bend crack
the silence of aging

when did she start writing in the margins
of someone else's story
where did she leave her voice her song her
own damn noise

she trundles around the house in the
morning
slashing cymbals in her grasp
leaning creaking bending crashing
the promise of aging

gun metal

gun metal sky
white capped sea

old growth trees in the park across the street
sun baked roots

low stone wall sand freckled
salty breeze

i am still
held in you
silver circled
the loneliest girl in the world

dapple-oceaned from all sides
cold green water rushing to greet me

white capped sky
silver backed sea
cradle me

Maple Avenue

you held my hand
all the way home
even when we stopped for soft serve cones at the
fluorescent McDonald's
I had lost a part of me
some competitive streak some inborn confidence
and you
seemed to know that only your hand could fill
that hole
not words or easy excuses rational reasons or
spite
so we held hands all the way to Maple Avenue
and I just knew that it would always be this way
I never counted on the in-between days
how addition could equal such subtraction
we were going to sit on a porch when we were
eighty--
countless husbands behind us
I miss that memory

9 789395 784115